An Answer to Parent-Teen Relationships

by
Norman Wright

Harvest House Publishers
Irvine, California 92714

Note: Before reading this book, it is recommended that you first read *An Answer to Communication* and *An Answer to Discipline*, both in this same Answer Series. The principles outlined in these two books form a foundation for the principles contained in this book.

AN ANSWER TO PARENT-
TEEN RELATIONSHIPS
© 1977 by Harvest House Publishers,
Irvine, CA 92714
Library of Congress Catalog Card
Number 77-75940
ISBN 0-89081-075-3

Printed in the United States of America.

AN ANSWER TO PARENT-TEEN RELATIONSHIPS

If you are looking for the magic answers that will solve all of the problems between parents and teen-agers, this book is not for you. Unfortunately, such a book has never been written! But if you are looking for some sound principles and suggestions that will enhance your relationship with your preteen and with your teen-ager, this book may help.

Many parents experience panic and frenzy when their stable child suddenly moves into the unstable transition stage of life called adolescence. Many of the common difficulties and anxieties would not occur if parents had prepared both themselves and their children for the changes that come with adolescence.

What is a family? What is a healthy family relationship? What should a family provide for its members? Before we consider a definition of the family, take the time now to write down your answers to the following questions. Each member of the family, if old enough, should write his or her answers on a separate paper without consulting the other. Be sure your teen-ager answers the questions, and then as a family share and discuss your answers.

1. If you were to describe or define your own family life with one word, what would the word be?
2. What strengths do you see in your own family?
3. What strengths do you see in each of the members of your family? Have you told them that you are aware of these strengths and appreciate them?
4. What goals do you have for your family life?
5. What do you think your family members would say about your family?
6. What do your family members do that makes you feel loved or valued?
7. What do you do that expresses your love toward your family?
8. What expectations do you think God has for your family? What expectations does God have for you as a family member?
9. What do you feel is a weak area in your family life?
10. What can you do to strengthen this weak area, and what can you do to help reach the goals you have for your family life?
11. What family rule do you feel is a good rule?
12. What family rule would you like to change?

Now let's consider a definition of "family." A family is an organism that provides an atmosphere of support and encouragement, along with positive opportunities for growth. These growth opportunities include enabling each person to come to a knowledge, understanding, and acceptance of himself. The family also helps each member acquire a positive self-concept. These are ideals or goals, but they are attainable. Family members are very involved with one another and affect one another whether they realize it or not. Each family member has the choice of providing positive or negative input to the other members.

The parents are responsible to create and stabilize the family atmosphere. The teen-ager should not set the tone for the family. Many parents say, "If only my son or daughter were different or would do what he should, we could be happy and satisfied again." Scripture does not teach that happiness or joy is conditioned upon the proper behavior of all family members. The teaching of James 1:2, 3 can be applied to the family situation. A parent's happiness or optimistic outlook on life does not have to be subject to the frequent mood or behavioral changes of his adolescent. I am not saying that it is easy, but it is possible.[1]

---

1. See the discussion of this problem in *An Answer to Worry and Anxiety* by the same author.

This definition of the family stresses the importance of the atmosphere being such that each person's self-concept can grow and develop as it should. Unfortunately, the atmospheres of many Christian homes are just the opposite. This other type of atmosphere has been called a ''depressogenic environment,'' for it can actually cause depression. It actually provides a model of what the family atmosphere should not be like.

A depressogenic environment fails to provide a person with adequate support to build his self-esteem. This is a violation of scripture:

''Fathers, do not provoke or irritate or fret your children — do not be hard on them or harass them; lest they become discouraged and sullen and morose and feel inferior and frustrated; do not break their spirit (Col. 3:21 The Amplified New Testament).

This atmosphere in the home actively undermines self-esteem and repeatedly activates emotions and conflicts which a susceptible person cannot handle without becoming depressed.

A look at several specific characteristics of this environment is very important to the discussion of the healthy development of an adolescent.

DISALLOWING INDEPENDENCE

This characteristic keeps an individual from finding some degree of independence while one or several members of the family seek to maintain control. If a teen-ager needs anything, it is an opportunity to become a self-sustaining, independent person able to make mature decisions for himself according to his own set of internalized values. But some parents do not want to let go and let grow. The young person might make the wrong decision or mar the reputation of the parents, and anyway it is just quicker and easier to "do it ourselves." But how can a young person grow or learn unless they have the freedom to try and fail and then try again and succeed according to their ability?

A major cause of low self-esteem in the teen-ager is a parent's negative reaction to the self that the teen-ager is trying to assert. Parents often disregard that self and try to replace it with an image of what they want the teen-ager to be. The result of this negative reaction by parents is guilt feelings in the teen-ager when he tries to express true feelings.

How can you encourage responsible independence in young people? This process should really begin in the child's preschool years. But if some of the principles have not been followed, they can still be implemented at this point. First, any child needs to know what is expected of him. He needs to know the limits for his behavior and the consequences for not staying within those limits. If a teen-ager is expected home at 12:00, he needs to know that 12:01 is considered late just as 12:30 is late and that the consequences will be enforced in both cases. If the rule has been established in advance that a violation of the curfew means losing driving privileges, and this has been written into the dating contract (discussed later in this book), very little need be said concerning the consequences.[2]

As a child grows it is important that the parents work with him to assist him in developing his own inner set of morals and standards. Far too many teens who come from Christian homes, have given verbal assent to their parents' or church's values but when they get away from their jurisdiction or away from the influence of home or church, they become very unstable when confronted with other value systems.

2. See *An Answer to Discipline* for further explanation of these principles.

How can a parent assist his teen-ager to develop his own standards? Three approaches have been noted, the first two of which are the most common and also the most ineffective. One approach is to shelter the child or teen-ager by controlling his environment, selection of friends, entertainment, reading material, and school (always placing him in a Christian school) in order to prevent the child from becoming contaminated by the wrong influences. This approach just does not work, for a child or teen will learn about the world one way or another. In many Christian schools the same problems exist that are found in other schools — perhaps not to the same degree, but the students still develop a cleverness in hiding any deviant behavior. Creating a protective cocoon will not work, for someday the person must emerge. Even if the protection has been successful, he will usually be even less prepared to deal with the realities of life.

A second ineffective approach to insuring moral values in a teen-ager is an overreaction technique — a constant critical, negative attack upon non-Christian standards or behavior. Whenever a belief or behavior appears in a magazine or newspaper, or on TV, dogmatic and belittling comments are made in the presence of the child. This is done in hopes that he will see the wrongness of the object being attacked. Too often, however, this can have just the opposite effect. Some teens simply tune out the overreacting parent and wait until they are away from home to pursue this different life-style. They nod assent when in the presence of their parents, but as soon as the opportunity presents itself, their own behavior begins to reflect what their parents have been preaching against. The parents cannot understand why their teen did not follow their teaching, for they were so consistent in pointing out the wrongness of this very life-style. Some teens begin to cleverly act out the forbidden life-style even while living at home.

A third method of attempting to build values in the life of a teen-ager has been labeled the "innoculation approach." As a child develops through the preschool and primary years, he is learning the parents' value system through example and open discussion. Upon reaching the later elementary grades (ages 9-11), he is old enough to begin this discussion process with the parents. Sometimes when a person is given a shot from a medical doctor to gain immunity against a disease, he is given a small dosage of that disease which enables him to resist it should he come into direct contact with it later. The same principle has been applied in the teaching of values to children.

Parents using this approach take the opportunity to engage their child in a discussion of opposing viewpoints. They talk with (not to) the child or teen about different value systems and they discuss the pros and cons and consequences of each. They give him small doses of these various points of view so that when the child comes face to face with them he is both aware of what they are and prepared to deal with them.

Often these discussions use a case study approach where different value systems can be applied to the problem being considered. Especially in the area of dating and sexual behavior, a teen-ager needs to know the what and why of his standards. He needs to have decided how to maintain his standards well in advance of situations in which someone else challenges his beliefs.[3]

Another method of assisting a teen in the development of responsible independence is to encourage him to earn his own money and pay for his own non-necessity items. Too many young people have been given so much that they have failed to grasp the reality of the hard work involved in the payment of material goods. They observe parents paying for most of their items with a credit card and develop their own

3. See *Revolution in Learning: From Birth to Six*, by Maya Pines for additional information on this approach.

philosophy of life based on this type of economic system. Constant credit card buying does not teach the inner discipline of the delay of rewards or satisfaction until a person has the means in hand to purchase the goods. (For the sake of safety, establishing a credit rating and using credit cards properly, are essential areas of training in today's society.) This attitude may be generalized into other areas of life such as the pursuit of education for a better vocational choice, sexual behavior, etc.

One learning experience that our daughter had when she was fourteen left quite an impression on her. She needed several items of clothing from a department store and we decided to have her walk to the store and purchase the clothing with money we had given her. She went with her list and the cash. Her reaction when she returned was interesting. One of her first comments was, "You know, thirty dollars doesn't buy very much does it! I had several items to buy on that list but before I finished the money was gone. Clothing sure is expensive, isn't it!" That experience taught her more than any lecture could have.

Recently, our daughter wanted a stereo with a record player and AM/FM radio for her own room. After discussing the price range for such equipment and looking around, we decided that when she bought one it could not exceed $160 and she would have to earn the first $100. That was not a problem because I had some simple secretarial work I needed to have done and I would rather pay her than someone else. I agreed we would pay the remainder provided she would read six books which I would choose for her to read. When all of these goals had been attained, we would then go out and purchase the stereo.

Four months later the money had been earned and five and a half books had been completed. A local department store had a sale on stereos and, even though half a book remained to be read, we went over and found what she wanted at a considerable savings. We purchased the set and took it home. But in keeping with the original agreement, we said she could listen to one record but would then have to complete the remainder of her last book. She sat there for three solid hours until the last book was finished and then she really could enjoy what she had worked for. Her stereo receives good care for she knows what it took to earn it!

Another approach to developing independence is to involve the teen-ager in setting standards for his behavior in crucial areas such as driving, dating, and sexual behavior. (Dating and sexual behavior are discussed later in the book.) Today, our daughter is fifteen-and-a-half. She is looking forward to obtaining her driver's license on her sixteenth birthday. During the first semester of her sophomore year we began discussing with her a standard of driving. We asked her to suggest several guidelines or rules that she felt ought to be followed when she used the car and we told her we would offer some suggestions also. These were written down and then we discussed them.

Here is the preliminary items we agreed on for her driving agreement. Prior to Sheryl's driving, we will put this into final form and all three of us will sign it indicating our commitment to this agreement as a standard for driving. For some reason, when people sign a paper or an agreement there is a greater commitment to follow the principles or conditions.

SHERYL'S DRIVING AGREEMENT

1. Before using either car I will ask if I can use the car and explain the purpose.
2. If I want to go somewhere for myself, my homework and piano practicing must be thoroughly completed.
3. During the first six months of driving with my own driver's license, the radio will not be used while driving.

4. During the school year I will be allowed to drive to church on Wednesday nights but cannot take anyone home without prior permission.

5. I will not allow anyone else to use the car under any circumstances.

6. I will be allowed up to thirty-five miles a week and after that I will pay for any additional mileage.

7. I will not carry more than five passengers at any time in the Plymouth nor more than three in the Audi.

8. Upon receiving my driver's permit I will be allowed to drive to church and local errands when either Mom or Dad is along. I will assist in driving for extended periods of time on our long vacations under all types of driving conditions.

9. I will not give rides to hitchhikers under any conditions nor will I accept any ride if I should have any difficulty with the car.

10. I will either wash the car myself or have it done once every three weeks.

11. I will pay half of the increase of the insurance costs and in case of an accident I will assume half of the deductible cost.

There will probably be some changes and additions before the final agreement is established, but perhaps this will serve as a model for your own situation and can be adapted for your use.

Over half of the items on this list were suggested by our daughter. As her father I added the word *thoroughly* to number two. I was the one to insist upon number three which is her least favorite one, but one she says she can live with. The reason for the rule is that too many times a radio is distracting and often played too loudly. Driving is a serious privilege and responsibility, and when one is just learning to be on his own he needs to give full attention to what he is doing to perfect his skills. On rule six our daughter gave herself only thirteen miles a week, so we expanded the amount of free mileage. Rule eight indicates a latitude and freedom for her practice driving experience before she gets her actual license. We travel a great deal in the summer and believe this will give her the experience of driving under varied highway, traffic, and weather conditions so she will be better equipped when she is on her own.

Even before this contract was agreed upon, she had earned half of the increase in the insurance rate by helping me paint our house this past summer. Have you ever painted a house with a fifteen-year-old daughter? It is quite an experience, especially when you are on the top of a ladder and she is below you with a roller full of paint, and you feel it being rolled up one leg and down the other! Or when she leans over the top of the roof with a sly grin and a brush full of paint and you look up and know what's going to happen next, but there is nothing that you can do to prevent it! The house was painted in spite of all the episodes. For her first time at painting, she did quite well.

All of these activities take time, effort, and patience. But they are necessary if a young person is to have the opportunity and environment in which he can develop independence. Our daughter is basically independent by nature, and our task is basically a matter of challenging her thinking and using her drive to help her make better and responsible decisions.

ENCOURAGING DEPENDENCY

A characteristic of an environment that will hamper the development of a healthy self-concept is the encouragement of a dependency that convinces an individual that he cannot possibly survive without the other person's emotional support. This encourages the feeling that he cannot make proper decisions without your involvement or constantly checking up on him. Some parents have a difficult time when their teen-ager is away at camp or on an outing. They call each day, maintaining this dependent relationship and in many cases embarrassing the teen.

UNDERMINING SELF-ESTEEM

Another way to foster this depressogenic environment is to give ambivalent messages that undermine self-esteem and prevent a legitimate self-defense. For example, "Sue I love you, in spite of the way you are" or "You are conscientious in some areas, but you sure need to improve in some others if you're going to make it." The area of grades or achievements can cause considerable damage if not approached in the right manner. "You did all right with these five A's, but how did you get a B in this subject? Good grief!" We live in an imperfect world and we as parents are imperfect. Standards are important but they must be realistic and attainable. Even the most consistent person will have an off day. The family is the place where failure and mistakes can be turned into learning experiences through mutual acceptance and encouragement.

How do your responses affect family members? Are they helped by the statements? Does your message give them insight on what they may have done that was wrong? Does it help them to do a better job next time? Telling a person that he is stupid because he can't pound a nail straight doesn't teach him to hammer it correctly. Yelling at one's daughter for being late or telling your friends about it in her presence doesn't help her to be on time.

The Word of God has an answer for this: "Stop being so critical of one another. If you must be critical be critical of yourself and see that you do not cause your brother to stumble" (Rom. 14:13, Phillips). The scripture also tells us to "encourage one another" (1 Thess. 5:14).

". . .criticism must be discriminate and take into account the fact that no human being is perfect and that there are many matters which are so unimportant that they should be ignored. . . .When criticism becomes indiscriminate it is called faultfinding and it leads to most destructive consequences. . . .

"[These] are the factors which make fault-finding so destructive. . . .

"1. Faultfinding is destructive because of its very definition. It is defined here in terms of communication as a way of saying: 'I do not accept you as a human being because I will not recognize in practice and in daily living that human beings are imperfect.' In other words, faultfinding expresses a lack of acceptance of people and a distorted view of reality.

"2. Because of the basic lack of acceptance involved, faultfinding ruins human relationships, makes people feel hostile toward each other, sours the daily atmosphere of the home and makes it a place of misery rather than of happiness and satisfaction.

"3. Faultfinding is destructive not only to the 'victims' (many of whom are not as innocent as it may appear), but to the faultfinder himself or herself, as well. That is because faultfinding makes the other person either turn you off completely or counterattack or store up resentment against you. . . .

"4. It follows that faultfinding is an ineffective method for changing the behavior of others. It may produce initial results, but if it is kept up it will lead to the other person not really hearing what you are saying; he may hear it in a mechanical sense but it will soon 'go out through the other ear.' Rest assured, however, that the lack of acceptance involved is received and understood.

"5. Thus faultfinding can be dangerous, because when the time comes that you have a truly necessary and important criticism to make, you are powerless then, having diluted the effectiveness of your arguments in advance so that they no longer mean anything to the person being criticized. The danger is especially apparent in the case of children who — through faultfinding — have been taught to think: 'Never mind, it's just that cranky old parent-faultfinder putting on his broken record again.'

"6. Faultfinding teaches unreasonableness and intolerance. Since it induces distaste it may lead the other party (spouse, child, employee, etc.) to become unreasonable in the other extreme by becoming especially careless and making an excessive number of mistakes, thus setting up a neurotic interaction. . . .

"7. Faultfinding is a consequence of reliance on certain destructive defense mechanisms. The typical faultfinder either projects his own shortcomings onto another person or displaces his anger toward one person (e.g., boss) onto another (e.g., wife). Most often faultfinding is an unconscious way of trying to hide one's weaknesses by projecting them onto someone else. . . ."[4]

Don't you have to be angry in order to get your point across to others? They don't seem to respond unless anger is a part of the message! Believe it or not, it is possible to share a complaint or a criticism with another person in a calm, well-thought-out manner that will bring

4. Sven Wahlroos, *Family Communication*, (New York, N.Y.: Macmillan, 1974), pp. 20, 21.

about more change than if you responded to him in anger. Many families find healthy problem solving to be a major area of dissatisfaction in their homes. Here are a few techniques which have worked for some. Perhaps these will help you avoid an angry explosion.

1. State the problem or complaint as soon as you can verbalize it. The longer you let the problem fester, the greater the possibility of resentment building and bitterness eroding the relationship.

2. Share your problem or concern in private so you don't embarrass the other person or cause him to feel that he must save face.

3. Let the person know that you are pleased with several aspects of the relationship before sharing what it is that bothers you.

4. Be sure to speak in the first person. Use "I statements" such as "I feel" and "I don't like to be" rather than "you are" and "you did this." "You statements" sound like accusations and quickly lead to self-defense and nonlistening and perhaps even counter-complaining.

5. Pinpoint the actions that concern you and don't become a mind reader focusing upon what you *think* the other person's motives are. Perhaps he was rude or didn't listen but do you really *know* that he had definitely planned to do that.

6. Comparing this person's actions and behavior with the failings of others does little to help solve the problems you are concerned about.

7. Forget the past. Talk about the present issue and make no reference to past difficulties.

8. Share only one complaint. It is too easy for the other person to feel dumped upon if he or she receives a barage of problems all at the same time.

9. Be sure to suggest in a non-angry, non-demanding, non-judgmental way some of the possible and realistic solutions that could be implemented.

10. Be sure you let the other person share his feelings and ideas about the problem that you are bringing to his attention. Even if he responds in anger to what you have said, his response is not reason for you to become angry. [5]

PROVOKING GUILT

Another problem of the faulty home atmosphere is the repeated provoking of guilt. This is

5. Adapted from John Lembo, *Help Yourself*, (Niles, Ill.: Argus Communications, 1974), pp. 40, 41.

done by making the other person feel responsible regardless of the facts. Statements to a teen
which convey the message that he is responsible
for the disruption of the family, the mother's
depression and worry, or the other children's
discouragement does not help him — it only
produces feelings of guilt which may just
compound the problems.

SUPPRESSING EMOTIONS

Another very serious characteristic is the
refusal to allow any open show of emotion and,
in particular, healthy reactions to anger. The
denial of our emotional life has very serious
consequences for us psychologically and physio-
logically. Emotions are a gift from God. He
created us with the capacity to experience them.
Teens need a healthy model of emotional
expression from their parents. Open discussions
of emotions and ways of expressing feelings can
be very beneficial for the teen.[6] Perhaps we
don't care for the way they express their
feelings. The appropriate time to discuss proper
ways of expressing themselves is when family
members have calmed down.

6. For additional information on assisting a young child, see Carl
   Fischer, *What About Me*, (Pflaum Standard Publishers). See also
   An Answer to Frustration and Anger, (Harvest House
   Publishers).

BLOCKING COMMUNICATION

A final characteristic of a depressogenic environment is the blocking of open and direct communication. We must communicate to live and to have quality relationships. Perhaps this cartoon reflects some parental beliefs about communication.

Communication is a process of sharing what you think, believe, or feel, both verbally and nonverbally in a way that the other person can both accept and understand what it is that you are sharing. Communication also includes listening to the other person — listening in such a manner that you are not thinking about what you are going to say when the other person finishes talking!

How is the communication between you and your teen? Would you like to improve it? Consider the following suggestions for enhancing the communication process.

A Communication Exercise for Teen-Agers
by Millard J. Bienvenu, Sr.

"This is a joint project for you and your son or daughter — an exercise in human communication. Many parents have found this exercise quite helpful in better understanding their teen-agers; it should also help teen-agers understand their parents. For many it has reopened blocked channels of communication or opened new channels. Before you begin the exercise, here are some suggestions:

"Explain to your teen-ager that his parents have been reading this. . . in an effort to better understand him (her). And that at this point there is a short exercise for him. It is designed to help all of you find out how well you communicate — or whether you fail to communicate — and how to improve certain aspects of your relationship.

"Reassure your son (or daughter) that his answers will be treated with confidence and respect.

"Promise to discuss and consider his answers with an open mind, trying to see things from his point of view; he need not fear punishment or retaliation if you disagree with his answers. The purpose is to learn more about what one another is thinking and feeling.

"Have your youngster thumb through the exercise, and when he is ready, allow him to answer the questions in private.

"1. This inventory is an exercise designed to help you and your parents better understand how you communicate with each other. Most teen-agers find it very interesting.

"2. There are no right or wrong answers. The most helpful answer to each question is your indication of the way you feel at the moment.

"3. The YES column is to be used when the question can be answered as happening *most of the time or usually*. The NO column is to be used when the question can be answered as *seldom or never*. Draw a circle around the word YES or NO, whichever reflects your answer.

"4. Read each question carefully. If you cannot give the exact answer to a question, answer as best you can but be sure to *answer each one*.

1. Do your parents wait until you are through talking before "having their say"?   YES   NO

2. Does your family do things as a group?   YES   NO

3. Does your family talk things over with each other?   YES   NO

4. Do your parents seem to respect your opinion?   YES   NO

5. Do your parents tend to lecture and preach too much to you?   YES   NO

6. Do you discuss personal problems with either of your parents?   YES   NO

7. Do your parents tend to talk to you as if you were much younger than you actually are?   YES   NO

8. Do they show an interest in your interests and activities?   YES   NO

9. Do you discuss matters of sex   YES   NO
with either of your parents?

10. Do your parents trust you?   YES   NO

11. Do you find it hard to say what   YES   NO
you feel at home?

12. Do your parents have confi-   YES   NO
dence in your abilities?

13. Do you hesitate to disagree   YES   NO
with either of them?

14. Do you fail to ask your parents   YES   NO
for things because you feel
they'll deny your requests?

15. Do they really try to see your   YES   NO
side of things?

16. Do your parents consider your   YES   NO
opinion in making decisions
which concern you?

17. Do they try to make you feel   YES   NO
better when you're down in
the dumps?

18. Do your parents explain their   YES   NO
reason for not letting you do
something?

19. Do you ask them their reasons   YES   NO
for the decisions they make
concerning you?

20. Do you help your parents to   YES   NO
understand you by telling
them how you think and feel?

Now complete these statements:

What worries me most about my future is

_____

_____

_____

The main weakness of American parents is

_____

_____

_____

The most difficult subject to discuss with my parents is _____

_____

_____

What I want most out of life is

_____

_____

_____

Now that you have finished the exercise, the next step is to discuss it with your parents as soon as the three of you are able to sit down together without any interruptions. Your parents should ask you why you chose the answers you did. The more you talk, the more they learn. Encourage them to continue similar discussions.'' [7]

By talking about the type of environment that a teen-ager *does not* need, I have also indicated some of the things he *does* need. He needs a family environment that provides a training ground for the development of inner discipline and responsibility. He needs an example of responsibility from a mother and father who behave and function on a rational, loving level with each other. The modeling of the parents will strongly affect the development of the teen.

He needs to learn the discipline and stamina needed to cope with life situations, especially those which do not go according to his own expectations. He needs to learn alternative actions and approaches to frustrating situations. He can learn this by the example of his parents as well as through instruction on how to discover different solutions to the various problems of life.

A teen-ager needs a family in which there is inner strength to cope with the difficulties of life as well as strength of convictions and values.

7. Millard J. Bienvenu, St., Parent-Teen-ager Communication, Bridging the Generation Gap, Public Affairs Pamphlet No. 438, (New York, N.Y.; Public Affairs Committee, 1969), used by permission.

When a child or teen finds compromise or vacillation in parental beliefs or standards, he will have a difficult time in building the foundations for his value system.

The importance of a positive self-concept has already been emphasized. One of the main goals of parents should be to see that their child develops into adulthood with a positive self-concept.[8] Parents greatly affect the development of the self-concept. If the teen's family values and loves him, his chances of developing are optimal. We value a person by recognizing him, his personality, and his uniqueness apart from his behavior or what he produces. His love and worth are not dependent upon his abilities or production level. What matters to the adolescent is not what others actually think of him but what he thinks they think of him. His perception or evaluation of their attitudes is important.

A teen-ager needs limits along with directions. This involves firm and loving discipline. Reports indicate that teens who come from homes in which there are limits and firm

8. Two excellent books on the subject of the development of a good self-concept are: Lloyd Ahlem, *Do I Have to Be Me?*, (Glendale, Ca.: Regal Books, 1973) and Maurice Wagner, *The Sensation of Being Somebody*, (Grand Rapids, Mich.: Zondervan, 1975).

discipline are less likely to become involved with drugs than teens who come from permissive backgrounds. When one knows the boundaries he feels a sense of security even though he may try to test the limits. Parents should accept the fact that when a teen is testing the rules and limits, this is normal behavior.

Dr. Roy W. Menninger has made some helpful suggestions that may help parents deal with some of the anxiety they feel as parents of teens. Consider these principles; they have helped others.

1. Don't let your feelings of inadequacy as a parent get you down. Every parent who is honest has moments of unsureness. The haunting question, "Am I handling this situation right?" will never go away. But the question itself is proof that you're functioning as a parent. As long as you keep asking it, things are far from hopeless.

2. Don't let a certain amount of friction in your family discourage you. Disagreement — even loud disagreement — is a form of communication. It's a dialogue, a bridge. Friction may be unpleasant, but it's a lot better than indifference or silence.

3. Don't be afraid to be yourself. You have your own values, your own life-style. Stick to

them, even if your children seem scornful or disapproving. They *want* you to be loyal to your own standards. They need a yardstick to test themselves by.

4. Don't mistake a passing personality phase in a youngster for a permanent problem. The other day a mother told me sadly that her 14-year-old daughter, who used to confide in her easily and naturally, had stopped doing so. No more friendly conferences. No more seeking of advice. Just a sudden turn-off.

   Is this natural? It is. The time always comes when the adolescent turns away and begins to look for values and guidance from his or her own peer group, as well as from other adults. This won't last forever. But the parent who fights it too hard can make everyone miserable.

5. Don't make permissiveness the scapegoat. It's fashionable nowadays to blame permissiveness for everything that seems wrong with the younger generation. This is a dangerous over-simplification because it implies that the remedy is the reverse: authoritarianism, repression, law-and-order. There has to be a limit-setting, to be sure. But one extreme is as bad as the other. Harshness just makes adolescents fight harder.

6. Finally, don't ever slam the door. At times, as every parent knows, the temptation can be strong. When a youngster seems endlessly hostile, sullen or unresponsive, it's easy — and very human — to react with anger and withdrawal. But the "difficult" child is often the one who needs your patience and understanding the most. . . . [9]

William Clark discusses what every teen has the right to expect from his parents and what every parent has the right to expect from his teen:

EVERY TEEN HAS THE RIGHT TO EXPECT:

1. A father and mother who love each other and show it daily — in small ways and big ways.
2. Two persons who place on their list of life's priorities God first, then each other, and their children next. . . .
3. Two interested, kind and loving guides. Two (not perfect, but) good examples.
4. Parents who put the relationship first, always — before rules, what others may think, etc.

---

9. Roy W. Menninger, M.D., "How to Understand the Perplexing Teen-ager," *Readers Digest*, March 1972, used by permission.

5. Enough time in the average week with parents (actually there, in person) to build a relationship. Regular times to talk (one-to-one).

6. To be allowed to be a teen-ager. The right to feel and think as an individual.

7. Expressed affection, appreciation and respect.

8. To be understood and feel understood. It is often difficult for parents to accept and understand why what is serious to parents cannot be as serious to teens. Keeping the house tidy, putting out the garbage is important, but not to teens.

9. Consistent, reinforcing acceptance. To be treated as a valuable, capable human being. Never being torn down, never being attacked personally.

10. To be listened to, always. (Not unhearing anger or patient endurance until you can, out of your vast, omnipotent fund of adult widsom, "tell them a thing or two.") Dialogue on issues where room for disagreement is valid. [*Only parents who have struggled and learned to communicate with each other will do so with their children.*]

11. Parents who never treat lightly what is important to a teen-ager.

12. An attractive home — one of order,

schedule and tranquility (that is, most of the time).

13. The right to privacy.
14. Guidance in forming good health habits. (Being overweight is more than just a physical burden to carry.) Provision of food, clothing; the basic physical needs.
15. Information about: God, the Bible, a relationship with Christ, life, worthy goals, values, standards, sex, morals, alcohol and drugs.
16. A single standard for both parents and the teens regarding alcohol, drugs, honesty, morals, church attendance, etc.

EVERY PARENT HAS THE RIGHT TO EXPECT:

1. Expressed affection, appreciation, respect and obedience.
2. Communication — to know how their teen feels.
3. An honest attempt by the teen to understand his or her parents' difficulties and areas of concern. (Their home, lawn, etc.; Mother's wide range of responsibilities; and the pressures on Dad that teens cannot feel.)
4. A thoughtful, serious consideration of parents' beliefs, values and standards.
5. Cooperation with all family members.
6. To be able to trust their teen-ager.

7. The teen taking responsibility for some tasks around the house.
8. To know where their teen-ager is and when he or she is to be home (to prevent parents' worrying, and to allow for their guidance; not because of lack of trust or confidence).
9. Participation in family times of prayer, reading and discussion.[10]

Consider these concepts as you reflect upon your own family life. To help increase the extent of your family communication and relationships, several activities are provided for you at the back of this book. You will find a series of discussion questions which can be used for family discussions or as conversation starters. You will also find an activity called Family Role Trading which could give considerable insight about how family members see one another.

DATING STANDARDS AND SEXUAL BEHAVIOR

Two major areas of concern which parents have are dating standards and sexual behavior. Preteens are included here because so much of the discussion and training needs to take place

10. From *Family* by William G. Clarke, (Marriage & Family Enrichment Institutes, 3502A Nebraska Ave., Tampa, Florida 33603, Copyright © 1975 by William G. Clarke), pp. C14-16, used by permission.

well before the teens reach the stage of dating. What do your preteens or teens believe about dating? What do they believe about sexual behavior on dates or prior to marriage? This next section will raise some questions and suggest several approaches which can be used in the context of the family.

How do you feel about the questions that teens are asking today about sex? As parents we need to be capable of answering these questions. We must also create and foster an atmosphere in which any question can be asked. Too often Christian parents thrust this responsibility onto the youth director or pastor of the church. In order to fulfill our responsibility we may have to go through an educational process ourselves to make sure we are knowledgeable. (At the back of the book you will find a bibliography of resources on the subject of sex for parents and teens.)

To test your ability to answer teens' questions concerning sex, read through the following questions which were asked by tenth and eleventh graders from evangelical churches at a senior high camp.

1. Isn't it true that if a girl has had sexual intercourse before marriage and later realizes she has sinned against God, and asks for forgiveness, that God accepts her

as a virgin? If this is so, should the girl once again think of herself, with God's help, as a virgin?

2. What's wrong with French kissing before engagement?

3. What do you think about marrying someone of another race?

4. Just how do you go about getting turned off if your girl has got you turned on?

5. On a scale of 1-10 how much is sex a part of a Christian marriage?

6. After marriage, when girls are having their periods, can they still have sexual contact?

7. If you had been raped by a male in your family should you tell your husband if he asks? Or should you just forgive and forget because you've talked it over with the Lord?

8. Why can't you feel a girl's breasts before marriage? The Bible doesn't say anything about it.

9. Do you think petting should be advisable when first going steady or when you are first engaged?

10. Is it right not to plan to marry if God wants you to get married, or should you expect to get married and then if you don't, accept it as God's will?

11. What exactly is "Sodomy"? Isn't there a law against it? What other sexual acts are illegal?

12. Is there anything wrong with having premarital oral sex?

13. I have recently found out that an older friend of mine is a homosexual. He is not a Christian but through my Christian witness, I feel God may be doing serious work in his life. Should I remain friends with him even though I know he is attracted to me?

14. What do you do when you're very much in love with a guy and he says he loves you but he thinks he's super stud and goes out on you? He says he feels rotten about it afterwards.

15. Do you think it's wrong to have sexual intercourse, even though you are in love with that person and would not break respect with one another?

If you had difficulty dealing with these, you may want to consult the material recommended in the bibliography for some of the answers. What do you do if your adolescent began asking you some of these questions at home? First, be thankful that he feels free enough to come to you and ask. Second, if you don't know the answer, don't fake an answer or say, "Ask your mom" or "Ask your dad" or "Ask the pastor." Tell him you don't know, but you will find out the answer.

What about helping your teen establish a standard for dating? Perhaps some of these suggestions will help you develop your own plan for what is right in your family. Here are some questions for both you and your teens to answer. Write down the answers on a separate sheet of paper and then discuss your answers together. It is essential to discuss your answers together as a couple first so you are in agreement.

Questions for Parents:

1. What qualities does your son or daughter have to offer a person he or she might date?
2. In which area do you trust your teen the most?
3. In which area do you still have some concerns and how do you plan to assist your teen to strengthen this area?
4. What qualities would you like to see in the person your teen dates?
5. Should your teen date just Christians or both Christians and non-Christians?
6. What dating activities are permissible and which ones would you not want him to become involved with?
7. What time do you feel your teen needs to return home after a date? Does it depend upon the activity? If so, explain.
8. How often can your teen date each week?
9. At what age will your teen be able to date? Will these be single dates or dates in a group?

10. If you have a daughter, will you ask to meet the boy before she dates him? If so, what would you discuss? What would you ask him?

11. Will you encourage your teen to bring his date to dinner or to visit or have parties at your home?

12. At what age do you feel comfortable about your son or daughter becoming engaged or marrying? Should he finish vocational training or college first?

13. Now go back over all these questions and attempt to answer them as you think your teen will answer them. You may need some time to discuss these questions with your spouse. You may have a class or group at church where you would like to discuss these questions with other parents.

Questions for the Teen:

1. At what age do you want to begin to date?

2. What is the purpose of dating?

3. What qualities in your life do you have to offer a dating partner?

4. What qualities do you want to see in a person you date?

5. What would you like to do on your dates and where would you like to go? Are there some types of dating activities that you feel you will not become involved in?

6. Do you want to date Christians or

non-Christians? Why?

7. How late should you be allowed to say out on dates? Does it depend on the activity? Explain.

8. How often should you be allowed to date each week?

9. At what age should you be allowed to date? Why did you choose that age?

10. How do you feel about your parents meeting the person you date? Should they meet him before you go out with him?

11. At what age do you want to become engaged? Marry?

12. How can you determine God's will about the person you will marry? What scriptural principles would help you?

13. How do you think your parents answered each of these questions?

The discussion you have following the completion of these questions may be a unique experience for you. You may discover that your philosophy of dating is similar or worlds apart. Two resources that will assist you in answering the question on God's will and marriage are the booklet *Dr. James Dobson Talks About God's Will*[11] and the tape "Christian Principles of

11. James Dobson, *Dr. James Dobson Talks About God's Will*, (Glendale, Calif.: G/L Publications, Regal Books Division, 1976).

Choosing a Mate.''12

Your dating standards may be different than those of the Christian family down the block, and different than some of the principles suggested here. This is fine. The important thing is that your standards are carefully thought through and your reasons are clear, both for yourself and your teen-ager.

Here is one example of a dating standard which was developed by a teen-age girl and her parents. Remember, as you and your teen-ager develop agreements like this, it is important for the teen to suggest his or her rules and guidelines along with the recommendations from the parents. Then the discussion and negotiations take place.

DATING COVENANT

1. I will have one date per week on either Friday or Saturday except for on special occasions. Sunday or Wednesday night activities are not considered a date.

2. I will be allowed to stay out until 10:30. Each event, however, will be discussed in advance and the time could vary depending upon the occasion. If I am late for any reason, I will call home.

12. David Seamands, ''Christian Principles of Choosing a Mate.'' A Tape Series available from Tape Ministries, P.O. Box 3389, Pasadena, Ca. 91103.

3. My parents will meet the fellow before I go out on a date with him.

4. If I know the boy very well, I will be able to start with a single date. If not, it will be a double date or group activity.

5. Since the purpose of dating is to establish a friendship and the possible selection of a future mate, I will date only Christian fellows.

6. I will let my parents know where we are going on our dates. All parties which I attend must have adult chaperones. Rock concerts and private dances are not allowed but school proms and sponsored socials are acceptable.

7. We may attend selected movies but I understand that most films we attend will have a "G" rating. These will be discussed with my parents and the films will be selected on the basis of Philippians 4:8.

8. If we would like to talk following a date, we may come into the living room but will not remain in the car. I understand that my parents will respect our privacy.

9. I will accept no blind dates.

10. I agree to memorize and be able to explain the meaning and application of the following versus before beginning to date:

I John 5:11,12   James 4:7,8

John 16:24

I Cor. 10:13

I John 1:9

Prov. 3:5,6

I John 5:14,15

Mat. 7:7,8

Eph. 4:29

I Thess. 4:3

Phil. 4:8

I John 5:4,5

I John 4:4

Eph. 6:10,11

I Cor. 15:57

Romans 8:28

I John 4:10

I Peter 1:15,16

Ep. 5:4 (Amplified)

Jer. 33:3

Isaiah 40:29,31

Isaiah 41:10

Isaiah 43:2

11. I agree to follow my standard for expressing affection which I have discussed with my parents.

As parents, my wife and I decided that our daughter can begin to date when she is sixteen. This does not mean that she has not had boy friends or been with them on activities. Sharing Church activities together as well as having boys coming over to our home to visit have all been part of her life, but actual dating has been delayed.

Her standard and ours is that she will only date Christian fellows. The biblical teaching of believers not marrying unbelievers can be used as a model for dating, since the underlying purpose of dating is eventually mate selection.

As parents, we feel that most movies, including the majority of PG-rated films, are not suitable fare for our minds and thought life, so attendance at these will be limited. Rock concerts likewise are out because of the atmosphere, environment and content of the songs.

What our daughter and your teen will do when they reach the age of eighteen will be a different matter. They should then be capable of making some of their own decisions. Some parents at that age take off all rules and restrictions. Others decide that as long as their child is living at home, the parents still have some say about his activities. Rules are a part of life and students at Christian colleges find that adherence to rules (even though they may not like particular rules or believe in them) is necessary.

Another area of concern is the type of person that our daughter will be dating. We have a high regard for our daughter and feel very positive toward her. (This does not mean that we are perfect parents nor is she a perfect daughter. We all have areas to change and strengthen in our life.) We want the best for her in her dating life and experience and we want to convey this to the young men who date her. We plan to meet the fellows prior to their date with Sheryl, and our daughter understands this. We want this to be an informal time of getting acquainted, but also a time to find out about the beliefs of the young man.

The subject of sexual behavior prior to marriage is an important topic. This is another area where we must assist our teens in establishing a healthy Christian standard of behavior. Sex is God-created and God-given, and He has designed it to be used in a certain manner.

Here is an interesting chart of sexual behavior which has been used during the past few years with youth and parents as well as by parents with their own teens. The examples on the chart indicate the various ways people express their affection to one another. The styles of sexual expression for four different couples has been indicated. The first couple engages in all of the various sexual activities very rapidly. The second couple leaves only sexual intercourse for marriage. They have done everything else and these individuals are sometimes referred to as "technical virgins." The third couple has gone as far as French kissing prior to marriage, and the last couple has engaged in kissing and left everything else for marriage.

This chart is explained by the parents to their teens who are then asked to take a piece of paper and draw what they feel their own standard should be in their dating life. Reasons for the standard should be given and discussed openly. Parents need to be careful not to be

SEXUAL BEHAVIOR

L = LOOK
T = TOUCH
h = HOLDING HANDS LIGHTLY
H = CONSTANT HOLDING HANDS
k = LIGHT KISS
K = STRONG KISS
K̃ = FRENCH KISS
B = FONDLING OF THE BREASTS
SO = SEXUAL ORGANS
SI = SEXUAL INTERCOURSE

FRIENDSHIP	DATING	GOING STEADY	ENGAGEMENT	MARRIAGE
TL	h HkKK̃B	SO SI		
TL	h H	k K	K̃ B SO	SI
TL	h Hk	K	K̃	B SO SI
TL	h H	K	K	K̃ BSOSI

shocked by some responses or to become angry or defensive if your standards do not coincide with your teen's standards. Unfortunately, teens today are more open and free with sexual expression than ever before. Prior to using this material with your teen, it is very important that you decide what you believe is an appropriate standard for yourself and for your teen. The four examples given are just examples; there are many other variations. The order, obviously, remains the same.

The books and tapes listed in the bibliography may appear to be more important to you now as you discover your need to spend time in preparation prior to engaging your teen in this discussion. Not only should this standard be completed by a teen when he begins to date and his reasons thought out, but he should know how to maintain the standard. Does he know the various lines a fellow or girl might use to manipulate a date into sexual activity? Does he or she know how to say no? Does he realize that a boy must be just as responsible for control as the girl? Too often the responsibility for control has been placed upon the girl, which allows the fellow to keep trying and then place the blame upon the girl. Dating couples have found that if there is open communication between them about their standards and ideals, and that they plan in advance not to become involved in situations that might cause difficulty, and that they are able to develop a way to tell the other immediately when they have reached their limit, standards can be maintained. The book *Why Wait?*, listed in the bibliography, offers additional help on this subject and should be read by your teens.

Some parents have said, "What if my teen asks me how far I went before I was married? What do I do then?" Honesty is very important. Some parents feel good about the standard they maintained. Others were not Christians or if they were, still went too far. A general explanation emphasizing the forgiveness of Jesus Christ and how the ministry of the Holy Spirit can be employed in one's own life will help at this point.

Bibliography of Resources on the Subject of Sex

Tapes
Wheat, Ed. "Sex Problems and Sex Techniques in Marriage." This series includes three hours of the finest and most complete discussion on the subject. It is for parents and married couples, not for teens.

Wright, H. Norman. ''Sex and the Bible.'' The two tapes in this series can be used with parents and teens for discussions and teaching. One message is a survey of the biblical teaching on sex. The other offers suggestions for helping adolescents develop a standard of sexual behavior, and includes a discussion of the chart of dating standards presented in this book. (Both series of tapes can be ordered from:

Christian Marriage Enrichment
8000 E. Girard
Denver, Co., 80231

Books

Hollis, Harry, Jr. *Thank God for Sex.* (Nashville, Tn.: Broadman Press, 1975). For parents.

Life Can Be Sexual. W. J. Fields, Editor, (Concordia Publishing House, 1967). For senior high students.

Miles, Herbert. *The Dating Game.* (Grand Rapids: Zondervan Publishing House, 1976).

Miles, Herbert. *Sexual Understanding Before Marriage.* (Grand Rapids: Zondervan Publishing House, 1971).

Scanzoni, Letha. *Sex Is a Parent Affair.* (Glendale, Calif.: G/L Publications, Regal Books Division, 1973). For parents.

Scanzoni, Letha. *Why Wait?* (Grand Rapids: Baker Book House, 1975). For parents, and senior high and college-age students.

W. J. Fields, Editor, *Take the High Road.* (Concordia Publishing House, 1967). For junior high students.

Study and Discussion Ideas

1. What do Proverbs 18:13 and James 1:19 mean for your family life?
2. Is it possible to disagree without quarreling? How?
3. If you were to put Galatians 6:2 into practice in your family, what would you do?
4. Discuss what kind of family vacation you would like to take this year.
5. In what ways do you show interest in your parents' or teens' interests or activities?
6. Do you discuss matters of sex with your parents or teens? Why? How do you feel about it?
7. Do your parents or teens help you to understand them by describing how they think or feel?
8. Describe the funniest thing that ever happened to your family.
9. What is the most embarrassing thing that has ever happened to you?
10. When a difference arises, are you and your parents or teens able to discuss it together? Explain your answer.

11. In what ways do you consider your parents' or teens' opinions in making decisions?

12. Do your parents or teens accept your reasons for the decisions you make?

13. How do you make your parent or teen feel better when he is down in the dumps?

14. Is it hard for you to say what you feel in talking to your parents or teens?

15. What were you thinking about when the last person was talking?

16. Tell the others what you plan to be doing ten years from now.

17. Should a wife and a mother have a career?

18. If you were to describe or define your own family life in one word, what would that word be? Why?

19. If a teen-ager obeys and respects his parents, will he always cooperate and be understanding?

20. What strengths do you see in your own family?

22. What do you feel is a weak area in your family life? Why? What can you do to strengthen it?

23. What do your parents or teens do to make you feel loved or valued?

24. What do you do to express your love toward your family?

25. In looking forward to marriage, are mutual interests more important than physical

attraction?

26. After a Christian couple are engaged, can they have more freedom in their sexual expression with each other than before?
27. On some occasions is it all right for a Christian to marry a non-Christian?
28. When love hits, does one know it?
29. Do you think everybody should marry? Why?
30. Do you believe that an argument is a destructive force in the home between parents and teen-agers?
31. Is quarreling always wrong for a Christian family, even if insights are gained thereby?
32. What is the wisest course to take when an argument seems to be developing? Remain silent? Leave the room?
33. What does "honor your parents" mean?
34. How does a father provoke his children to wrath and resentment?
35. Tell your parents or teens something you always wanted to say.
36. When was the last time you cried and what did you cry about?
37. If you were to ask your parents or teens to pray about something, what would it be?
38. A good rule in our home is. . . .
39. A rule in our home that I would like to change is. . . .
40. Parents are best when. . . .

41. What is your goal in life?
42. Who has influenced you the most spiritually?
43. I wish my church would. . . .
44. I wish my children would. . . .
45. I wish our family were not. . . .
46. I wish more than anything that. . . .
47. Define nagging. Why do people nag? What could they do in place of it?
48. I wish our home were. . . .
49. Should an adolescent always obey a parent without questioning what he says or his authority?
50. Do you think parents should have a voice in who their son or daughter dates?
51. Will teen-agers take responsibility when they are ready to do so?
52. Do you agree that most of the problems between parents and teens occur because the parents fail to listen or understand the teen?
53. Describe the ideal teen-ager.
54. What are the major problems facing teen-agers and what can be done to deal with them?
55. Describe what you like to daydream about.
56. What do you want said about you when you have died?
57. Describe how you feel about yourself.
58. What makes you like yourself? What makes

you dislike yourself?

59. What qualities in Jesus would you like to have in your life?

60. In what ways does Christ make a difference in your family life?

A SAMPLING OF SCRIPTURE PASSAGES REFERRING TO SEX AND FAMILY

Genesis 1 and 2— Creation of male and female

Genesis 1:26-28 — Sex relations in marriage

Genesis 26:8 — Sex play before intercourse

Genesis 38:9 — Avoiding conception

Genesis 39:9 ff — Fornication

Exodus 22:16-17 — Seduction

Exodus 22:19d — Bestiality

Leviticus 18:23

Leviticus 18:22 — Homosexuality

Leviticus 20:13 — Incest

Leviticus 20:10 — Adultery

Deuteronomy 22:23-27 — Rape

Book of Hosea — Hosea's marriage to a harlot and his subsequent forgiveness is likened to the relationship between God and Israel as Israel plays the harlot and breaks her covenant with God.

I Samuel 2:22 — Temple Prostitution

II Samuel 11-12 — David and Bathsheba (Lust)

II Samuel 13 — Annon and Tamar (Lust)

Proverbs 5:18-20 — Rejoice in your wife

Proverbs 23:27-28 — Prostitution

Song of Solomon — Love poetry regarding Bride and Groom

Matthew 5:27-28 — Adultery, Lust (Scripture silent on masturbation; this passage could relate)

Matthew 10:35-36 — Family Relationships

Romans 1:19-27 — Sex deviations (e.g., Homosexuality)

I Corinthians 6:9, 10, 15-25 — Adultery

Matthew 15:19 — Fornication

I Corinthians 7:2-9 — Marriage

I Corinthians 7:5 — Abstinence

I Corinthians 7:10-11 — Divorce

Matthew 5:31, 32; 19:3-9

I Corinthians 11:8-9 — Woman created for man, submits freely and in joy to her husband

Galatians 5:19-21 — Punishments for immorality

Ephesians 5:5 — No immoral or impure man has any inheritance in the kingdom of God.

Ephesians 5:25 — Love of husband and wife

Ephesians 5:28-33 — Love of husband and wife

Colossians 3:18 — Instruction to wives

I Timothy 5:10-14 — Advice to mothers, widows

I Peter 3 — Instruction to wives and husbands

I John 4:7-11 — Love for one another

Family	Marriage
Genesis 1:28: 2:24	Genesis 2:24
Deuteronomy 6:1-25	Matthew 19:5,6
Psalms 127:3-5; 128:3	John 2:1-11
Ephesians 5:22-6:9	I Corinthians 7
Colossians 3:18-25	Ephesians 5:22-23
	I Thess. 4:1-8

WHAT THE BIBLE SAYS ABOUT SEX

Sex	Old Testament	New Testament
	Sex is good in God's sight	Sex is approved
	Sex for pleasure is approved	
	Sex play is recognized as normal	
	Sex is openly discussed	Inferred
Fornication	Forbidden	Forbidden
Adultery	Forbidden	Forbidden
Harlotry	Forbidden	Forbidden
Masturbation	Nothing stated	Nothing stated
Homosexuality	Forbidden	Forbidden
Bestiality	Forbidden & condemned	
Incest	Forbidden	Forbidden
Rape	Forbidden	
Sex thoughts		Lustful thoughts should be controlled

Family Role Trading at the Dinner Table

Purpose: To provide family members the opportunity to express how they see and understand other family members acting and reacting in various family situations and attempt to enhance empathy for each other.

Ideal Group Size: This exercise is designed for use by individual families in their own home.

Time Required: Whatever time it takes a family to complete its dinner meal and conversation.

Material Needed: Sheets of paper or cards on which family members can identify the particular role that they will be playing.

Physical Setting: This exercise is designed for use by individual families in their own home around the dinner table.

Process:
   Step I: Have each youth participant assume the role of one of the other family members, with the adult members of the family attempting to take on the role of one of the youth members in the family. If there are more than two youth participants in the family, they can change roles with a

brother or sister.

Step II: In these reversed roles each participant is to carry out his role with regard to anything that happens at the dinner table; i.e., how he eats, what he eats, what he talks about, how he responds to what others do, etc.

Step III: After the dinner meal is completed, family members should discuss the results in the light of the following questions:

1. How did you feel in your assumed role?
2. At which points did you see yourself in the other person?
3. How do you think you would have behaved differently?
4. What did you learn about yourself? About the other person?
5. How do you now feel toward the person with whom you switched roles?
6. How will you go about trying to resolve any negative feelings regarding yourself that you may have discovered?

This exercise may be continued in other kinds of settings beyond the dinner table. For example, persons may want to continue in assuming their role positions for the remainder of the evening, sharing together in such activities as washing the dishes, clearing the dinner table, watching television, playing games, etc.[13]

13. Reprinted by permission of the Department of Christian Education, Christian Church (Disciples of Christ) and the Board of Christian Education, Church of God.

NOTES